Copyright Kim Sorgius 2015.

ALL RIGHTS RESERVED. This book contains material protected under International and Federal Copyright Laws and Treaties. Any unauthorized reprint or use of this material is prohibited. No part of this book may be reproduced or transmitted in any form or by any means, electronic or mechanical, including photocopying, recording, or by any information storage and retrieval system without express written permission from the author / publisher.

Unless otherwise indicated, all Scripture quotations are from The Holy Bible, English Standard Version® (ESV®), copyright © 2001 by Crossway, a publishing ministry of Good News Publishers. Used by permission. All rights reserved.

All Scripture quotations marked (KJV) are from The Holy Bible, King James Version. Public Domain.

The purchaser of this ebook has permission to print unlimited copies of the ebook text and journal for immediate family use only. For any group consisting of more than one immediate family, each family is required to purchase a copy of this ebook.

TABLE OF CONTENTS

O Come, O Come, Emmanuel

O Little Town of Bethlehem

Away in a Manger

Silent Night

Hark, the Herald Angels Sing

Joy to the World

We Three Kings of Orient Are

God Rest Ye Merry, Gentlemen

HOW TO USE THIS BOOK

I have written this unit study with the older elementary student (3rd-5th grade) in mind. Should you so choose, this study can be done fairly independently. For younger students, simply work together, allowing him/her to take control of any parts that can be handled independently. Of course, you may choose to do this study as a family and that would work perfectly as well!

Each hymn includes the music and lyrics for you to sing and learn. There is also a tin whistle tablature. This fingering would work for any similar instrument, like a recorder. Copywork is included for each hymn, both in KJV and ESV. These are located in the appendix for easier printing. Simply choose the translation that you prefer and then slip them into the right sections. Each section is labeled with the hymn name at the bottom.

Adaptations for a younger child-
Underline the section of copywork that your child can handle. I have purposely put a longer passage there for older kids, but you don't have to use it as is. Have your child copy what is appropriate for him/her.

In places where they are asked to write out a scripture, you might write every other word and have them fill in the missing words.

A few resources for biblical truth about Jesus' birth:

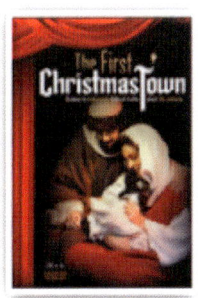

I used this video in the unit study. It is a wonderful resource. However, it is not mandatory for completing this study. You can use the Answers in Genesis site instead. If you are interested in purchasing it, click on the photo.

This cheerful computer "game" is filled with fun Christmas facts, merry music, and colorful images—all designed to teach the truth about this wonderful holiday and the traditions surrounding it.

O COME, O COME
Emmanuel

"O Come, O Come, Emmanuel" is probably the oldest Christmas hymn. Its lyrics come from the Advent events of the medieval Christian church. Each night, for seven nights before Christmas, the church would sing one of the "Great O Antiphons"-anthems sung to a short verse.

The word antiphon implies that the lines of each anthem were sung alternately by two choirs sitting opposite each other in the chancel. Each antiphon featured a prayer beginning with "O Come" and included an Old Testament reference for the Messiah.

JOHN MASON NEALE

About the twelfth century, five antiphons were put together as verses of a single hymn and a chorus was added, creating the words for "O Come, O Come, Emmanuel." In 1851, John Mason Neale translated this hymn from Latin to English, originally beginning "Draw nigh, draw nigh, Emmanuel." A year later, he changed the opening lines to "O Come, O Come, Emmanuel," the well-known words we use today.

Beautiful arrangements to listen to: Irish Whistle, Piano/cello, Choir.

©Not Consumed 2015 | Gloria: A Christmas Hymn Study

MY HYMN NOTES

Hymn Name
_____

Author
_____

Date Written
_____

Its original language was
_____

Other Facts
_____
_____
_____
_____
_____
_____
_____

Tell a little about the story behind the hymn. You can write and draw.

©Not Consumed 2015 | Gloria: A Christmas Hymn Study

O Come, O Come, Immanuel

Text: Latin, 12th cent.; composite
Tune: *Processionale*, 15th cent.; adapt. Thomas Helmore, 1854

1. O come, O come, Immanuel, and ransom captive Israel that mourns in lonely exile here until the Son of God appear.
2. O come, O Wisdom from on high, who ordered all things mightily to us the path of knowledge show and teach us in its ways to go.
3. O come, O come great Lord of might, who to your tribes on Sinai's height in ancient times did give the law in cloud and majesty and awe.
4. O come, O Branch of Jesse's stem, unto your own and rescue them! From depths of hell your people save, and give them victory o'er the grave.

Refrain
Rejoice! Rejoice! Immanuel shall come to you, O Israel

5. O come, O Key of David, come
and open wide our heavenly home.
Make safe for us the heavenward road
and bar the way to death's abode.

6. O come, O Bright and Morning Star,
and bring us comfort from afar!
Dispel the shadows of the night
and turn our darkness into light.

7. O come, O King of nations, bind
in one the hearts of all mankind.
Bid all our sad divisions cease
and be yourself our King of Peace.

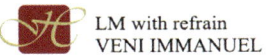

LM with refrain
VENI IMMANUEL

www.hymnary.org/text/o_come_o_come_emmanuel_and_ransom

This hymn is in the public domain. You may freely use this score for personal and congregational worship. If you reproduce the score, please credit Hymnary.org as the source.

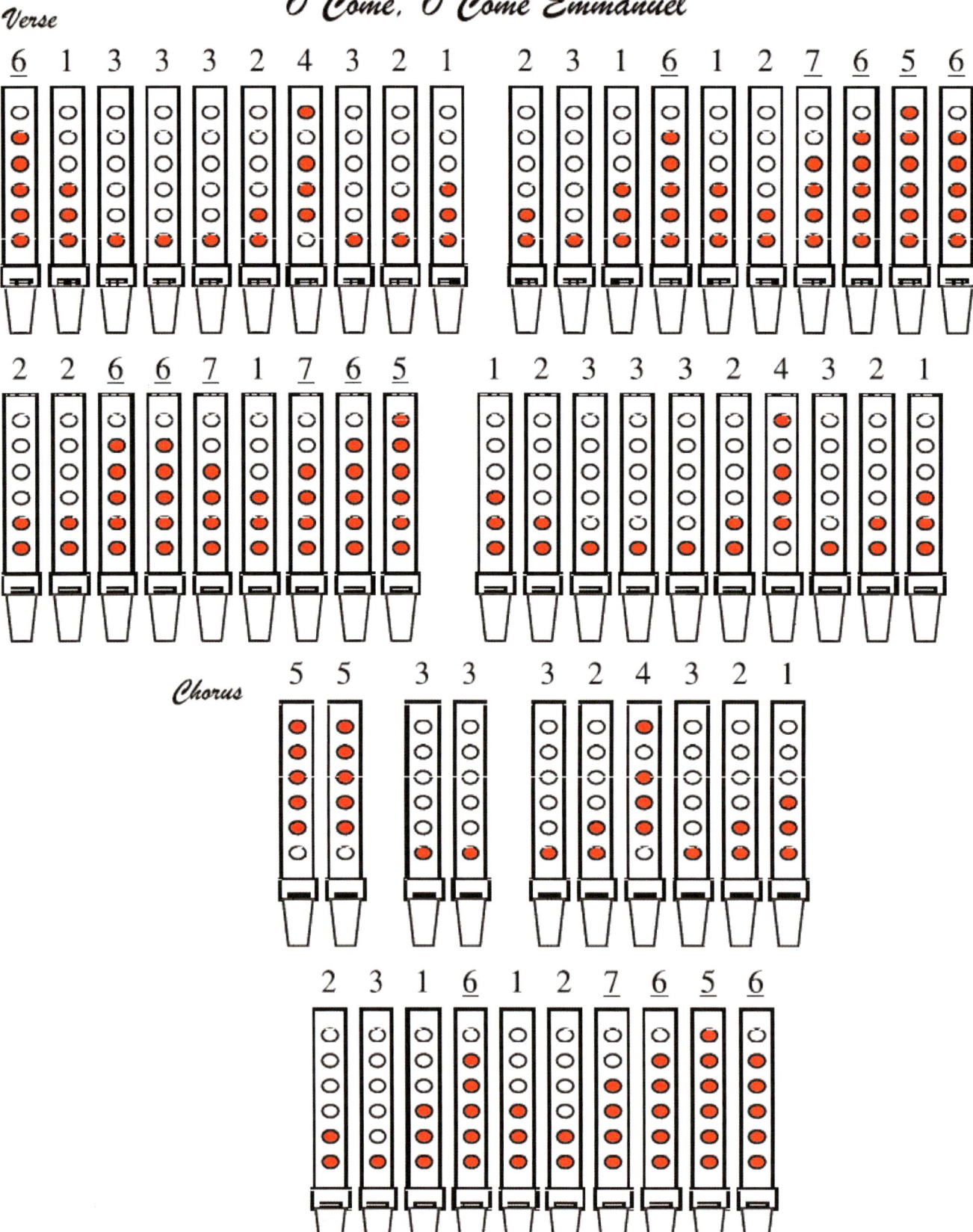

COPYWORK

O come, O come, Emmanuel
And ransom captive Israel
That mourns in lonely exile here
Until the Son of God appears
Rejoice! Rejoice! Emmanuel
Shall come to thee, O Israel.

Look up the hymn's five antiphons, which are Old Testament references to the coming Messiah. Match with the images on the next page.

Emmanuel (God with Us) Isaiah 7:14

Rod (Branch) of Jesse Isaiah 11:1,10

Dayspring (Morning Star) Numbers 24:17

Adonai Lord of Might Exodus 19:16

Key of David Isaiah 22:22

©Not Consumed 2015 | Gloria: A Christmas Hymn Study

Color and cut out. Then use with previous page.

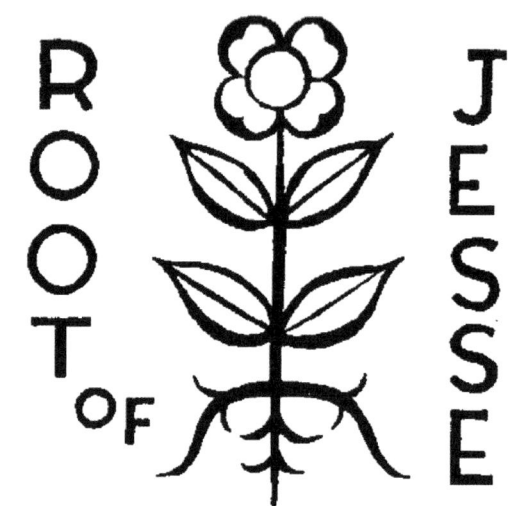

©Not Consumed 2015 | Gloria: A Christmas Hymn Study

How did the people become so desperate for a Savior? Start in Genesis and draw a timeline of all the events that you can remember since creation. Draw each event on a sheet of paper and cut it out. Then glue onto a long strip and paste onto this page. Keyword hints: Fall, Patriarchs, Egypt, Wilderness, Promised Land, Kings, Babylon. See this Timeline if you need help.

Read Isaiah 9:6. Using fun letters and colors write the names of Jesus that you find in this verse. You may use other names that you know as well.

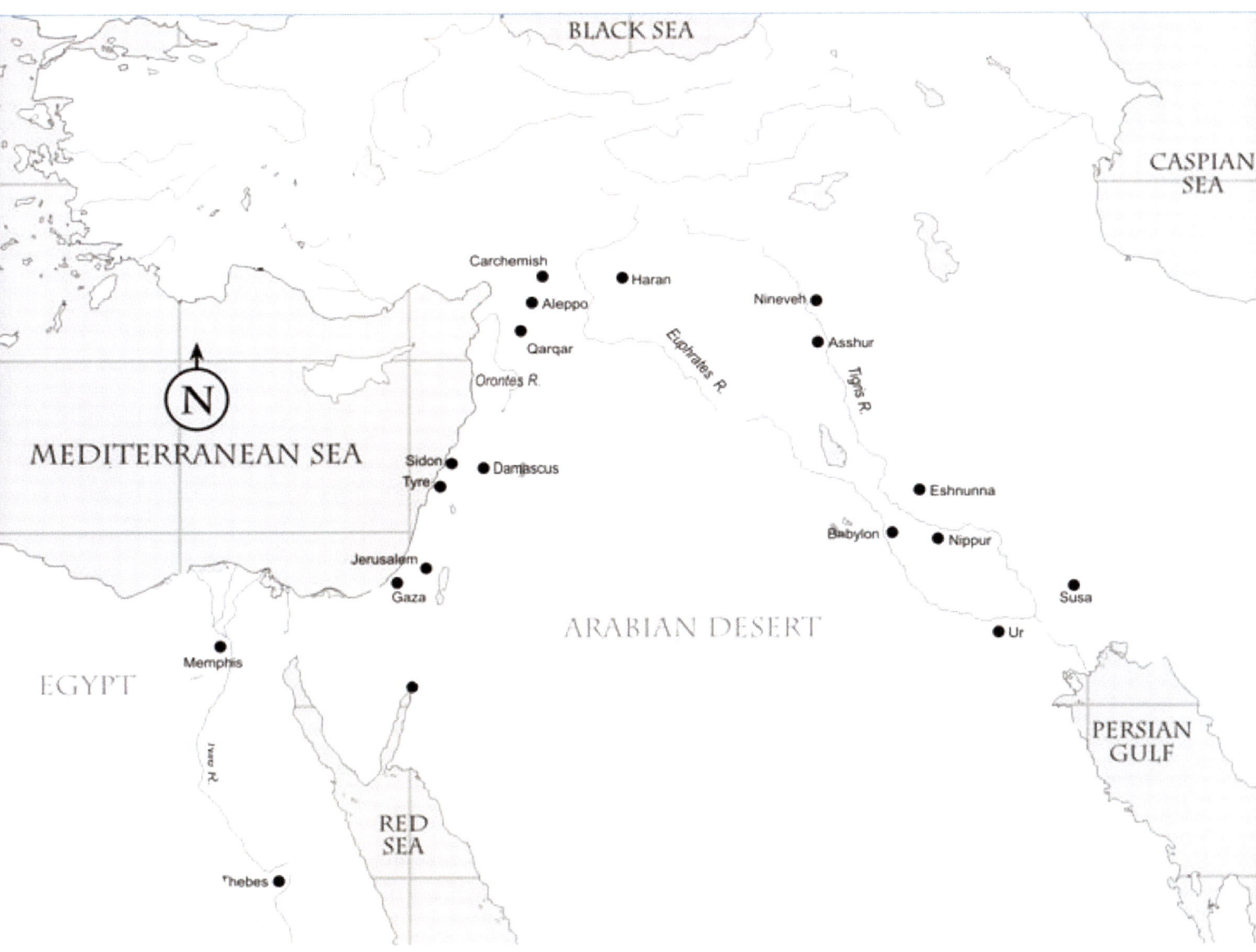

Using your timeline, mark the places as you tell the history of the Old Testament.

Make sure you mark:
- ☐ Ur, Abraham's home (see this map)
- ☐ Egypt
- ☐ Red Sea
- ☐ Promised Land
- ☐ Judah and Israel
- ☐ Babylon
- ☐ Jerusalem

MOSES AND THE TABLETS OF THE LAW, COSIMO ROSSELLI 1439 – 1507

From the time of Moses until today, the one major problem with God's people remains the same. What do we keep doing wrong? What can you do in your life to avoid this major sin? Read Judges 10:10 and 2 Chronicles 7:14.

_____

_____

_____

_____

_____

_____

_____

Not even 200 years old, "O Little Town of Bethlehem" has a much different story than our previous hymn. The lyrics were inspired by a horseback ride into the countryside on Christmas Eve in 1865. American pastor Phillip Brooks was deeply moved by the sight of the sweet little town and the shepherds in the fields as he traveled to preach at a service that evening. As he drifted slowly over the countryside, thoughts of our Savior's birth touched his heart.

When he returned home to Philadelphia, he penned the beloved words that we know today. Three years later he gave them over to his organist, Louis Redner, who put the lyrics to music for a Christmas service at Holy Trinity Church.

PHILIP BROOKS

Redner later shared these words about the event: "As Christmas of 1868 approached, Mr. Brooks told me that he had written a simple little carol for the Christmas Sunday-school service, and he asked me to write the tune to it. The simple music was written in great haste and under great pressure. We were to practice it on the following Sunday. Mr. Brooks came to me on Friday and said, 'Redner, have you ground out that music yet to "O Little Town of Bethlehem"?' I replied, 'No,' but that he should have it by Sunday. On the Saturday night previous my brain was all confused about the tune. I thought more about my Sunday-school lesson than I did about the music. But I was roused from sleep late in the night hearing an angel-strain whispering in my ear, and seizing a piece of music paper I jotted down the treble of the tune as we now have it, and on Sunday morning before going to church I filled in the harmony. Neither Mr. Brooks nor I ever thought the carol or the music to it would live beyond that Christmas of 1868."

Watch this great video on the story of O Little Town of Bethlehem and its author.

Listen to these beautiful arrangements: Vienna Boys Choir, Piano, Flute Choir

MY HYMN NOTES

Hymn Name
_____

Author
_____

Date Written
_____

Its original language was
_____

Other Facts
_____
_____
_____
_____
_____
_____

Tell a little about the story behind the hymn. You can write and draw.

O Little Town of Bethlehem

1. O little town of Bethlehem, how still we see thee lie!
   Above thy deep and dreamless sleep the silent stars go by.
   Yet in thy dark streets shineth the everlasting Light;
   the hopes and fears of all the years are met in thee tonight.

2. For Christ is born of Mary, and gathered all above,
   while mortals sleep, the angels keep their watch of wondering love,
   O morning stars, together proclaim the holy birth,
   and praises sing to God the King, and peace to all on earth.

3. How silently, how silently the wondrous gift is given!
   So God imparts to human hearts the blessings of his heaven.
   No ear may hear his coming, but in this world of sin,
   where meek souls will receive him still, the dear Christ enters in.

4. O holy Child of Bethlehem, descend to us, we pray;
   cast out our sin, and enter in; be born in us today.
   We hear the Christmas angels the great glad tidings tell;
   O come to us, abide with us, our Lord Emmanuel.

Text: Phillips Brooks (1835-1893)
Tune: Lewis H. Redner (1831-1908)

86 86 76 86
ST. LOUIS
www.hymnary.org/text/o_little_town_of_bethlehem

This hymn is in the public domain. You may freely use this score for personal and congregational worship. If you reproduce the score, please credit *Hymnary.org* as the source.

TIN WHISTLE TABLATURE

O Little Town of Bethlehem

Tablature copyright © 1999, John S. Atchley

Phillips Brooks / Lewis H. Redner

2
For Christ is born of Mary,
And gathered all above
While mortals sleep, the angels keep
Their watch of wond'ring love
O morning stars, together
Proclaim the holy birth!
And praises sing to God the King,
And peace to men on earth

3
How silently, how silently,
The wondrous Gift is giv'n!
So God imparts to human hearts
The blessings of His heav'n.
No ear may hear His coming,
But in this world of sin,
Where meek souls will receive Him still,
The dear Christ enters in.

4
O holy Child of Bethlehem, Descend to us, we pray; Cast out our sins and enter in, Be born to us today. We hear the Christmas angels The great glad tidings tell: Oh, come to us, abide with us, Our Lord Emmanuel!

COPYWORK

O little town of Bethlehem
How still we see thee lie
Above thy deep and dreamless sleep
The silent stars go by
Yet in thy dark streets shineth
The everlasting Light
The hopes and fears of all the years
Are met in thee tonight

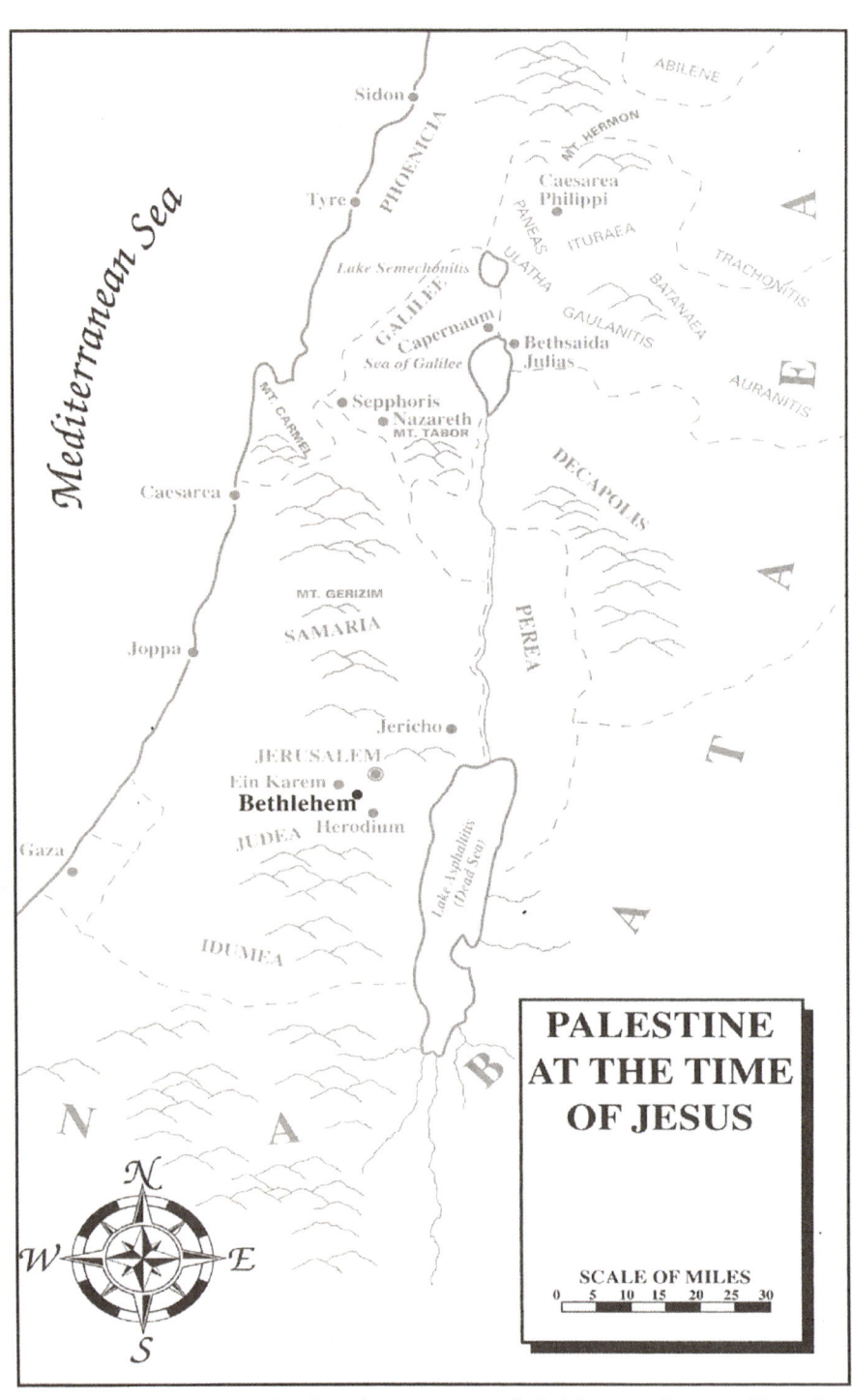

Find the town that Mary and Joseph were from. Read Luke 2:1-4.

Trace their journey on your map.

The journey was 80 miles, which probably took them about a week to walk!

Watch this video that shows what the walk might have been like.

What do you think the journey might have been like for Mary and Joseph?

_____

_____

_____

_____

THE ENTRY INTO JERUSALEM, GIOTTO c.1305

Now that Mary and Joseph are here in Bethlehem, how do you think they feel? What do you think was the first thing they did in town? Do you think their family had a celebration to welcome them?

___

___

___

___

___

___

___

What is Bethlehem like today?

Read this article: Bethlehem and answer the questions.

What does the word Bethlehem mean?

_____

In addition to Jesus, who else was born in Bethlehem?

_____

Name two other Old Testament events that occurred in Bethlehem.

_____

_____

_____

Describe Bethlehem today.

_____

_____

_____

_____

_____

Go on a tour of the Church of the Nativity in Bethlehem. Then draw something you learned or enjoyed.

Help Mary and Joseph get to
Bethlehem

©Not Consumed 2015 | Gloria: A Christmas Hymn Study

AWAY IN A Manger

Few Christmas songs are as loved as this tender children's carol. The author of this late 19th century German hymn is unknown. For some time, "Away in a Manger" was titled "Luther's Cradle Hymn." It was thought to have been written by Martin Luther for his own children and then passed on by German mothers. However, modern research shows that this may not be true.

Stanzas one and two first appeared in the Little Children's Book For Schools and Families, published in Philadelphia in 1885. The third verse was written by a Methodist minister, John T. McFarland, in the early 1900s when an additional stanza for this carol was desired for use at a church children's day program.

The tune of the song is not universal; indeed, over forty different tunes have been placed alongside the lyrics in hymn books. In the USA the main tune used with the lyrics is James R. Murray's 1887 "Mueller."

While the words to this hymn point our hearts
toward the miracle of such a sweet baby, "Away in a Manger's" lyrics may not be fully biblically accurate. The Bible does not say for certain that cattle were at the birth, nor does it say that Jesus did not cry as a baby.

Beautiful arrangements to listen to:
Organ, Piano, Choir

JOHN T. MCFARLAND

©Not Consumed 2015 | Gloria: A Christmas Hymn Study

MY HYMN NOTES

Hymn Name
_____

Author
_____

Date Written
_____

Its original language was
_____

Other Facts
_____
_____
_____
_____
_____
_____

Tell a little about the story behind the hymn. You can write and draw.

Away in a Manger

1. A-way in a man-ger, no crib for a bed, The lit-tle Lord Je-sus laid down His sweet head; The stars in the sky looked down where He lay, The lit-tle Lord je-su, a-sleep on the hay.
2. The cat-tle are lo-wing, the Ba-by a-wakes, But lit-tle Lord Je-sus, no cry-ing He makes; I love Thee, Lord Je-sus! look down from the sky, And stay by my cra-dle til mor-ning is nigh.
3. Be near me, Lord Je-sus, I ask Thee to stay Close by me for-ev-er, and love me, I pray; Bless all the dear chil-dren in Thy ten-der care, And fit us for hea-ven to live with Thee there.

Text: St. 1,2, anonymous, 1885;
st. 3, John Thomas McFarland, 1851-1913
Tune: James R. Murray, 1841-1905

11 11 11 11
MUELLER
www.hymnary.org/text/away_in_a_manger_no_crib_for_a_bed

This hymn is in the public domain. You may freely use this score for personal and congregational worship. If you reproduce the score, please credit *Hymnary.org* as the source.

©Not Consumed 2015 | Gloria: A Christmas Hymn Study

TIN WHISTLE TABLATURE

Away in a Manger

James R. Murray

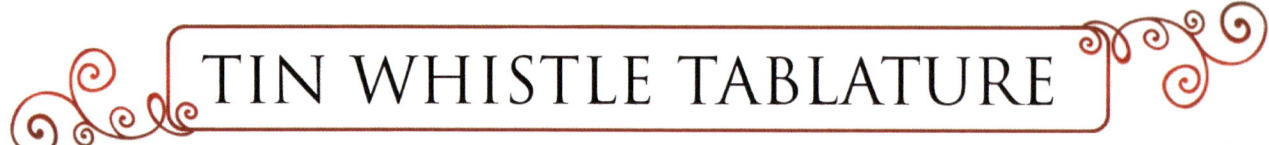

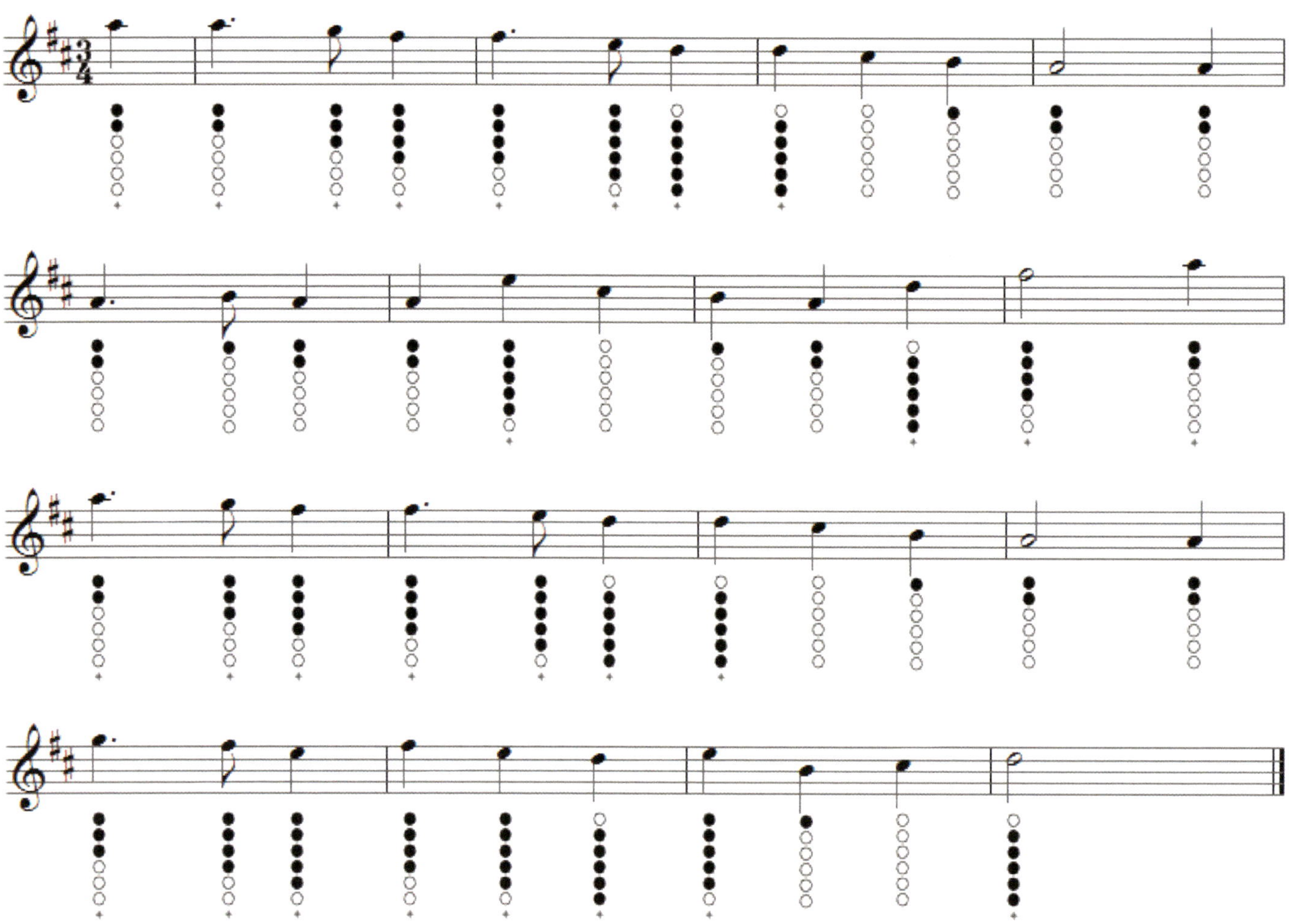

 | Gloria: A Christmas Hymn Study

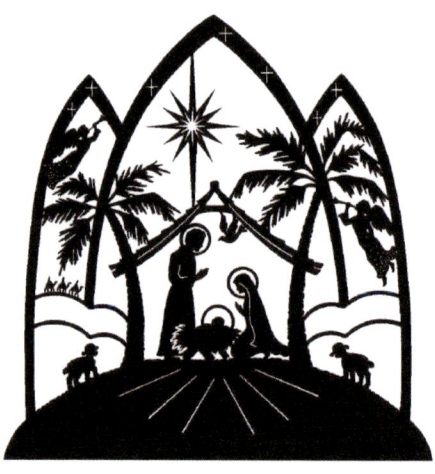

COPYWORK

Away in a manger, no crib for a bed
The little Lord Jesus lay down His sweet head
The stars in the bright sky look down where He lay
The little Lord Jesus asleep on the hay
The cattle are lowing, the Baby awakes
But little Lord Jesus, no crying He makes
I love Thee, Lord Jesus, look down from the sky
And stay by my cradle till morning is nigh

The Christmas Story...What Really Happened?

As thousands of years pass beyond an event, people often begin to remember the event differently in their minds. This is especially true with the story of the birth of Jesus. Many people have told this story with songs, pictures, words, and even plays. The story has changed quite a bit from what God's Word actually says. Let's take a look.

Was Jesus really born in a stable? Fill in the chart below with your ideas and then watch The First Christmas Town video. (If you did not download the full video, you can watch this video clip by Answers in Genesis: No Room for an Inn and/or read Born in a Barn by Tim Chaffey, Answers in Genesis.)

Fill in the chart below using words or pictures.

THE STORY	WHAT I THINK	WHAT THE BIBLE SAYS
How did Mary get to Bethlehem?		
Where did they stay in Bethlehem?		
How long was it before the baby was born?		
Were there animals with them when Jesus was born?		
Where did Jesus sleep?		

©Not Consumed 2015 | Gloria: A Christmas Hymn Study

ADORATION OF THE SHEPHERDS, GERARD VAN HONTHORST, 1622

Read about the shepherds in Luke 2:8-21. Write about what you think it must have been like to have been there at the manger that night.

_____

_____

_____

_____

_____

_____

_____

_____

And she gave birth to her firstborn son and wrapped him in swaddling cloths and laid him in a manger, because there was no place for them in the inn.
Luke 2:7 (ESV)

This beloved hymn has roots back to the year 1818. In the small Austrian village of Oberndorf, the church's organ wasn't working and would not be repaired before Christmas. (Note: some versions of the story point to mice as the problem; others say rust was the culprit.) Because the church organ was out of commission, actors presented their Christmas drama in a private home. That Christmas presentation of the events in the first chapters of Matthew and Luke put assistant pastor Josef Mohr in a thoughtful mood. Instead of walking straight to his house that night, Mohr took a longer way home. The longer path took him up a hill overlooking the village.

From that hilltop, Mohr looked down on the peaceful snow-covered village. Reveling in the majestic silence of the wintry night, Mohr gazed down at creation and remembered a poem he had written a couple of years before. That poem was about the night when angels announced the birth of the long-awaited Messiah to shepherds on a hillside.

So the next day, Mohr went to see the church organist, Franz Xaver Gruber. Gruber only had a few hours to come up with a melody which could be sung with a guitar. However, by that evening Gruber had managed to compose a musical setting for the poem. It no longer mattered to Mohr and Gruber that their church organ was inoperable. They now had a Christmas carol that could be sung without that organ.

In 1863, nearly fifty years after being first sung in German, "Silent Night" was translated into English by John Young. Eight years later that English version made its way into print in Charles Hutchins' Sunday School Hymnal. Today the words of "Silent Night" are sung in more than 300 different languages around the world.

Watch this video on the story behind Silent Night

Listen to beautiful arrangements here: German, Orchestra, Violin

MY HYMN NOTES

Hymn Name
_____

Author
_____

Date Written
_____

Its original language was
_____

Other Facts
_____
_____
_____
_____
_____
_____
_____

Tell a little about the story behind the hymn. You can write and draw.

Silent Night! Holy Night!

1. Silent night, holy night! All is calm, all is bright
'round yon virgin mother and child; holy infant, so tender and mild, sleep in heavenly peace, sleep in heavenly peace.

2. Silent night, holy night! Shepherds quake at the sight, glories stream from heaven afar, heavenly hosts sing alleluia; Christ, the Savior, is born! Christ, the Savior, is born!

3. Silent night, holy night! Son of God, love's pure light, radiant beams from thy holy face, with the dawn of redeeming grace, Jesus, Lord, at thy birth, Jesus, Lord, at thy birth.

Text: Joseph Mohr (1792-1848);
tr. John F. Young (1820-1885)
Tune: Franz Gruber (1787-1863)

Irregular
STILLE NACHT
www.hymnary.org/text/silent_night_holy_night_all_is_calm_all

This hymn is in the public domain. You may freely use this score for personal and congregational worship. If you reproduce the score, please credit *Hymnary.org* as the source.

©Not Consumed 2015 | Gloria: A Christmas Hymn Study

TIN WHISTLE TABLATURE

Silent Night

Music by Franz Xaver Gruber

COPYWORK

Silent night! Holy night!
All is calm, all is bright
Round yon virgin, mother and child
Holy infant so tender and mild
Sleep in heavenly peace
Sleep in heavenly peace

BENEATH THE SNOW ENCUMBERED BRANCHES, JOSEPH FARQUHARSON (1901)

"All was silent" according to the writer of this hymn. Can you imagine how you might have felt after waiting so long for a Savior? What do you think you would do and say if you had met Him that night in the manger?

_____

_____

_____

_____

_____

_____

_____

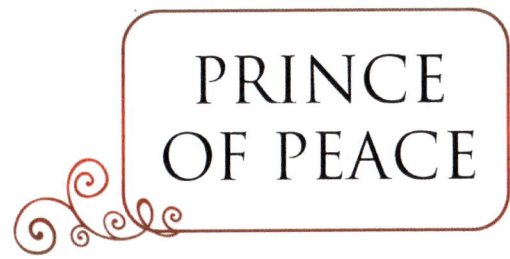
PRINCE OF PEACE

Although we often imagine that night as a silent one, the Bible doesn't say that baby Jesus didn't cry. But Isaiah 9:6 does say that Jesus would be the Prince of Peace. Let's look in the Bible and see what is meant by this peace.

Read Isaiah 32:17-18. What will we gain as God's people because of the peace that He gives us?

_____

_____

_____

How can we have peace? Write Isaiah 26:3 here.

_____

_____

_____

The Bible promises peace, but it doesn't say that we won't have trouble. Read John 16:33. Why do we have hope in times of trouble?

_____

_____

_____

Read Philippians 4:6-7. The verse says that God's peace will guard our hearts and minds. What must we do? (verse 6)

_____

_____

_____

SILENT NIGHT WORD SEARCH

```
H U V J L X B T L C A P Q Z N P E A C E
X G S Q V O Y B A A Z A H K W O D Z W Z
J V Z R B F L N A L Z F C O X W A X J P
Z Y M N L N P Z R M S X G O L V M F R C
O D Z D X S K N G M E T Y O O Y K E K P
B W U M W G H S T K C Q B B A Q B S P G
E O L N O X H L S C S M Y U D N D X J L
V S B U B T Q B Z U Q Y K Q V I F H J G
C I I U D L H S S Q E R I P G G Z X P C
Y L R E W U H E X B D Q J I B H D B I A
Y E T G I L J C R G C B B S S T R R R Q
X N H G I Q D K P J N F R N X E S I Z C
T T Y E I N U E W C H I L D G I X G L O
E M J I B Q D K L V N D K N B M A H W G
Q S I F K K V L X O L J A U A X G T I V
I F U U E J Z D G A O M N A O O B F Y R
G Y S F O T L O W S R M D X V T X I C S
O B U J R F R R H K D I Z I I N E Z X R
N M F L W N N D C C R N P H L Y V V J G
O S F Z I I N F A N T K H E A V E N L Y
```

CALM	BRIGHT	MANGER
SILENT	NIGHT	VIRGIN
HOLY	PEACE	MOTHER
CHILD	INFANT	HEAVENLY
JESUS	LORD	BIRTH

©Not Consumed 2015 | Gloria: A Christmas Hymn Study

This hymn has sparked much controversy. The form that we know today is very much not the way the original writer wrote it. In fact, he was angry when the changes were made to his hymn because the changes did not accurately share the story of Jesus according to the Bible.

You see, in 1739, John and Charles Wesley published Hymns and Sacred Poems, which included Charles' "Hymn for Christmas-Day." This hymn featured familiar lines such as: "Peace on Earth, and Mercy, mild, GOD and Sinners reconcil'd! Joyful all ye Nations rise, Join the Triumph of the Skies." But it did not begin with the familiar opening line, "Hark! the herald angels sing, Glory to the newborn King." In fact, the original Wesley carol began, "HARK how all the Welkin rings, Glory to the King of Kings." No herald angels to be found here!

The word welkin means vault of heaven. It's a word we don't hear much today, but it's the word that Mr. Wesley intended to use. You see, the story does not say that angels were singing when Jesus was born. This part of the song came into play when 18th century evangelist George Whitefield decided that the word "welkin" was unfamiliar and needed to be changed.

Over time, Whitefield and other editors changed the hymn to the lyrics we sing today.

Listen to these beautiful arrangements:
Organ, Saxophone Quartet, Choir

©Not Consumed 2015 | Gloria: A Christmas Hymn Study

MY HYMN NOTES

Hymn Name
_____

Author
_____

Date Written
_____

Its original language was
_____

Other Facts
_____
_____
_____
_____
_____
_____

Tell a little about the story behind the hymn. You can write and draw.

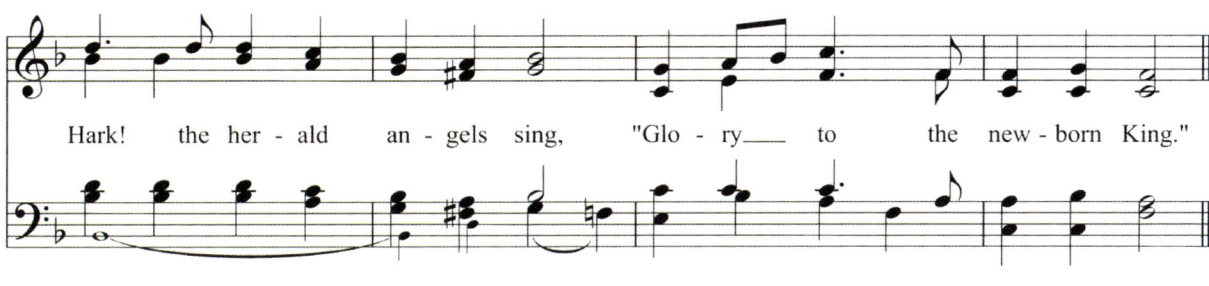

TIN WHISTLE TABLATURE

Hark! The Herald Angels Sing

Music by Felix Mendelssohn

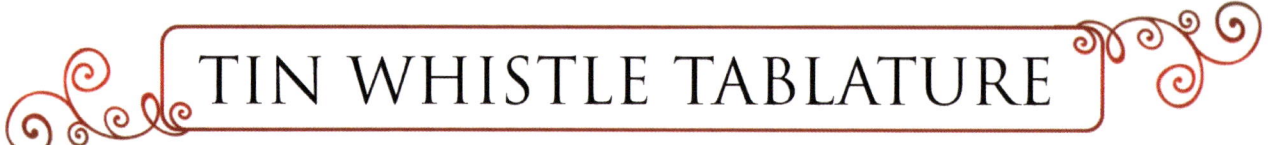

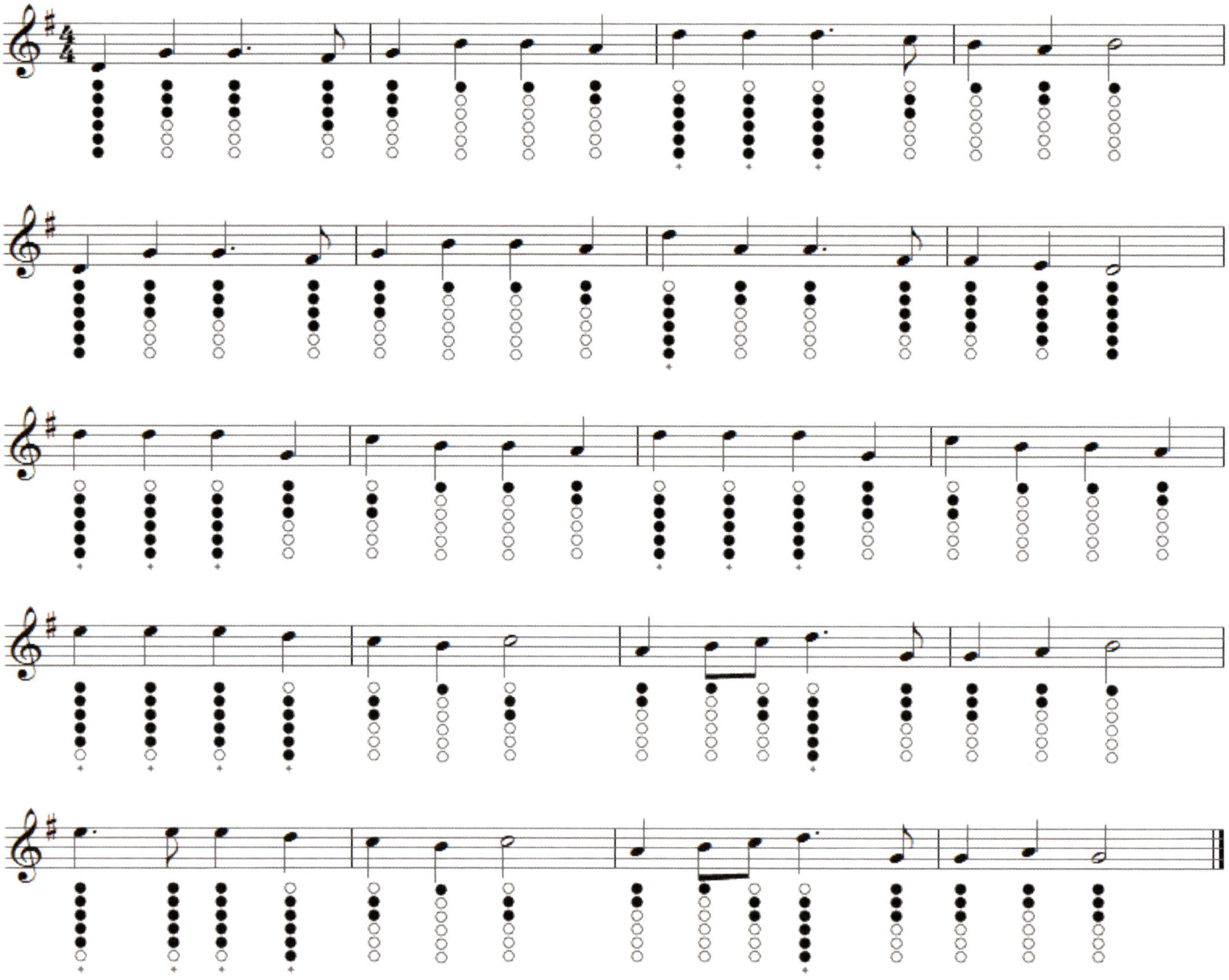

COPYWORK

Hark! the herald angels sing
"Glory to the newborn King
Peace on earth and mercy mild
God and sinners reconciled"
Joyful, all ye nations rise
Join the triumph of the skies
With the angelic host proclaim
"Christ is born in Bethlehem"
Hark! the herald angels sing
"Glory to the newborn King!"

ANGELS IN THE BIBLE

In the story of Jesus' birth, there are many times that angels appear. Let's look in the Bible for them.

Passage	Who was the angel talking to	What was said
Matthew 2:13-15		
Matthew 2:19-20		
Luke 1:8-17		
Luke 1:26-38		
Luke 2:8-14		

Read Luke 2:13. What word is used to describe what the angels did?

_____

Notice that it doesn't actually say they SANG praise. It's certainly possible, and maybe even likely, that they did but the Bible doesn't tell us this.

©Not Consumed 2015 | Gloria: A Christmas Hymn Study

DO NOT FEAR

Almost every time the angels appeared in the story of the birth of Christ, they said the same phrase. Write it here:

_____

Hopefully you wrote "do not fear" or "do not be afraid." God doesn't want us to be afraid. In fact, the Bible says not to be afraid over 365 times!

What things are you afraid of? Draw or write them in the box.

God gives us an excellent reason to not be afraid. Write Deuteronomy 31:6 here:

_____

_____

_____

HARK! THE HERALD ANGELS SING
WORD SEARCH

```
                        D  B
                        R  O
                     W  G  I  N
                     W  T  M  S
                  S  S  I  F  G  E
                  I  A  H  T  S  Y
   I  A  L  Y  A  B  R  L  Y  S  N  L  P  G  M  S  D  G  W  L
   R  A  H  B  T  H  C  C  I  O  N  N  N  E  K  E  E  S  U  J
   R  A  A  C  O  R  S  I  E  B  I  H  V  L  B  E  F  K
      U  J  R  E  E  T  V  F  K  E  O  I  M  C  Y  Y
         P  M  K  A  A  T  R  L  I  C  N  A  O  K
            A  N  E  S  M  H  E  N  R  E  J  O
            L  N  H  O  S  T  G  O  O  P  E  A  Q  P
            G  G  H  M  E  N  C  B  R  P  H  N  N  R
            L  M  E  R  B  I  E  W  J  O  R  R  G  G  N  P
            M  I  L  Z  S  R  E        X  H  L  E  P  L  M
         C  T  L  I  W  F  N           Z  T  L  M  P  O  D
      Z  J  D  C  O                          S  D  Z  O  R
   V  A  J  P                                         G  R  Z  Y
   Y  X                                                        Q  G
```

ANGELIC	HEAVENLY	NEWBORN
ANGELS	HOST	PEACE
BETHLEHEM	JOYFUL	PROCLAIM
CHRIST	KING	RECONCILED
GLORY	MERCY	RISE
GOD	MILD	SING
HARK	NATIONS	

©Not Consumed 2015 | Gloria: A Christmas Hymn Study

And suddenly there was with the angel
a multitude of the heavenly host praising God, and saying,
Glory to God in the highest, and on earth peace,
good will toward men.
Luke 2:13-14 KJV

"Joy to the World" was written by Isaac Watts (1674-1748), author of around 750 hymns. He was called "The Father of English Hymnody" not only because he wrote so many, but because he completely changed the way the church sang the Psalms when he published his book Hymns and Spiritual Songs. A few of his most well-known songs still sung today include: "Come Ye that Love the Lord," "When I Survey the Wondrous Cross," "At the Cross," and of course, "Joy to the World."

"Joy to the World" was written in 1719 and based on the last half of Psalm 98. If you notice the lyrics of the song, you will see nothing about shepherds, a manger, wise men, angels, or any other character or element that we normally associate with the Christmas story. Why? Isaac Watts did not write "Joy to the World" to be a Christmas song. The original theme of this song was the second coming of the Lord.

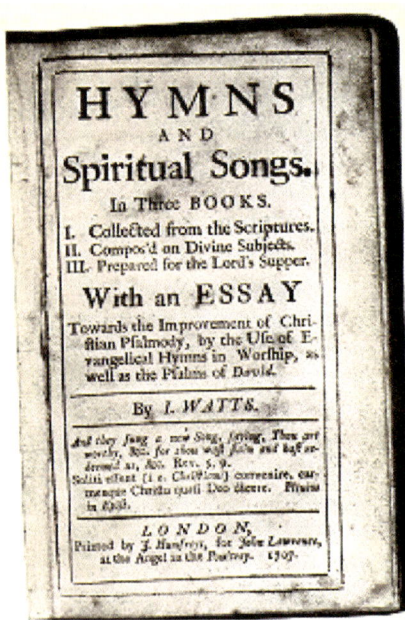

Over 100 years later, in 1839, Lowell Mason adapted and arranged this song into a melody many believe to have been written by Handel. It was at this time that "Joy to the World" became known as a Christmas song.

Listen to beautiful arrangements here:
[choir/orchestra](), [brass](), [children's choir]()

MY HYMN NOTES

Hymn Name

Author

Date Written

Its original language was

Other Facts

Tell a little about the story behind the hymn. You can write and draw.

Joy to the World! The Lord Is Come

Text: Isaac Watts, 1719; based on Psalm 98
Tune: Lowell Mason, 1848

1. Joy to the world! the Lord is come: let earth receive her King. Let every heart prepare him room, and heaven and nature sing, and heaven and nature sing, and heaven, and heaven and nature sing.

2. Joy to the earth! the Savior reigns; let all their songs employ, while fields and floods, rocks, hills, and plains repeat the sounding joy, repeat the sounding joy, repeat, repeat the sounding joy.

3. No more let sin and sorrow grow nor thorns infest the ground; he comes to make his blessings flow far as the curse is found, far as the curse is found, far as, far as the curse is found.

4. He rules the world with truth and grace, and makes the nations prove the glories of his righteousness and wonders of his love, and wonders of his love, and wonders, wonders of his love.

CM with repeats
ANTIOCH
www.hymnary.org/text/joy_to_the_world_the_lord_is_come

This hymn is in the public domain. You may freely use this score for personal and congregational worship. If you reproduce the score, please credit Hymnary.org as the source.

©Not Consumed 2015 | Gloria: A Christmas Hymn Study

TIN WHISTLE TABLATURE

Joy to the World!

Tablature copyright © 1999, John S. Atchley

Isaac Watts / George Frederick Handel

2
Joy to the earth! The Savior reigns; Let men their songs employ; While fields and floods, rocks, hills, and plains Re –
peat the sounding joy, Repeat the sounding joy Repeat, repeat the sounding joy.

3
No more let sins and sorrows grow, Nor thorns infest the
ground; He comes to make His blessings flow Far
as the curse is found, Far as the curse is found, Far
as, far as the curse is found

4
He rules the world with truth and grace, And makes the nations
prove The glories of His righteousness, And
wonders of His love, And wonders of His love, And
wonders, wonders of His love.

©Not Consumed 2015 | Gloria: A Christmas Hymn Study

COPYWORK

Joy to the World! the Lord is come
Let earth receive her King
Let every heart prepare Him room
And heaven and nature sing
And heaven and nature sing
And heaven, and heaven and nature sing

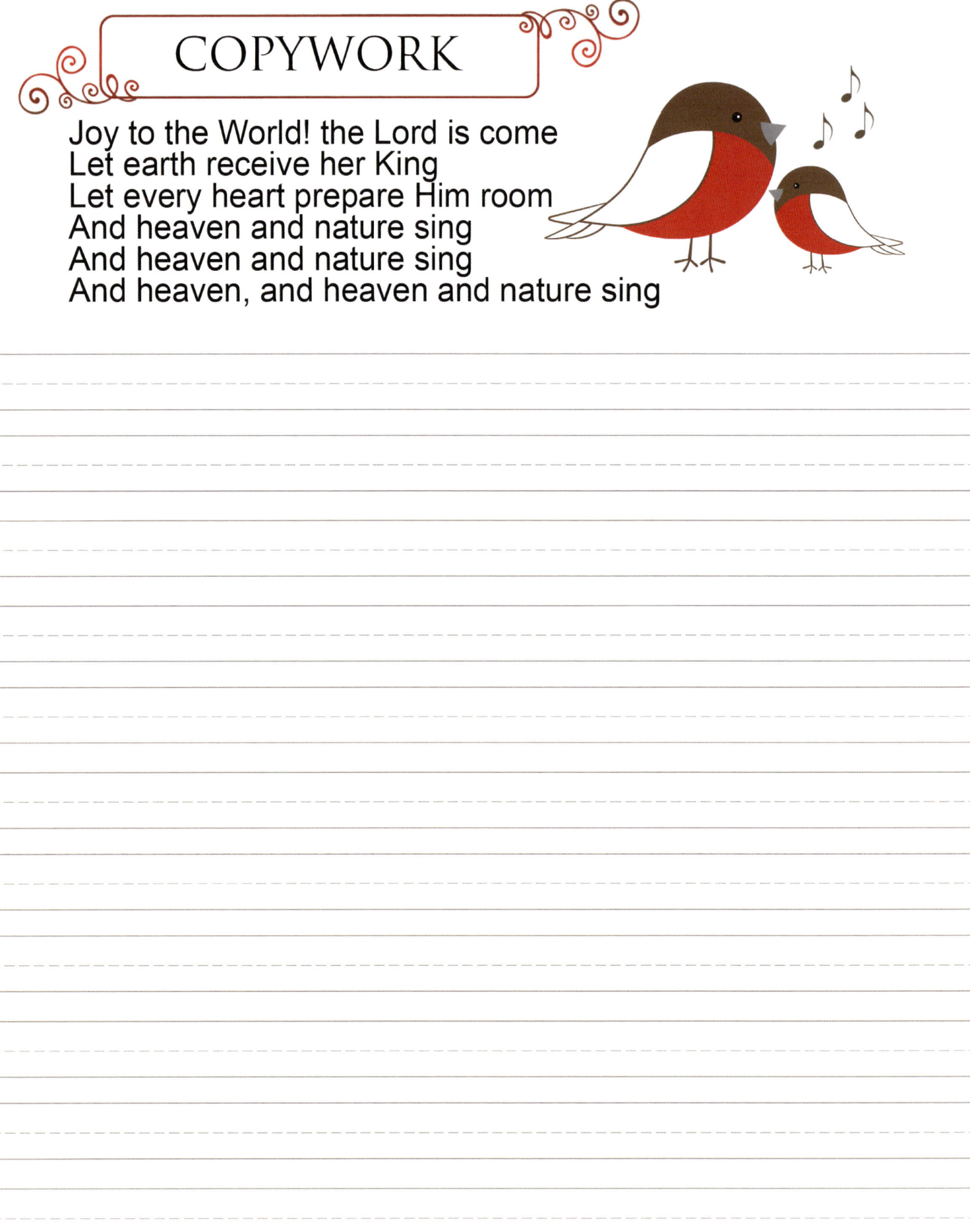

The lyrics in "Joy to the World" say, "Let every heart prepare Him room." This implies that there is something we need to do to make room for Jesus in our lives. James 1:21 says that we need to put off all filthiness and rampant wickedness so that we can receive the Word of the Lord.

In the cross below, list some things that you need to "put off" or stop doing. With Jesus, you can stop doing these things so that you can focus on Him.

In the heart, write the word JESUS.

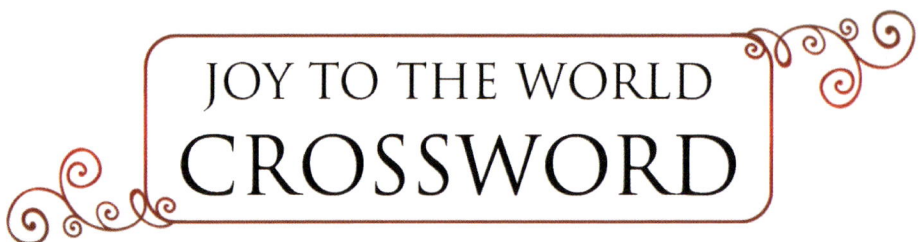

JOY TO THE WORLD CROSSWORD

Complete the crossword below. Use the Bible (ESV) or the lyrics to the song to help you.

Across
3. According to Philippians 4:4, what should we rejoice in?
4. Joy is a fruit of the _____. Gal 5:22
7. Prov. 17:22 says that a joyful heart is good _____.
8. In Romans 15:13, who fills us with joy?
11. The kingdom of God is for _____ and peace and joy. Rom. 14:17

Down
1. Joy to the _____
2. Let earth receive her _____.
5. 1 Peter 1:8 says that we will have _____ joy.
6. Be joyful _____. 1 Thessalonians 5:17
9. For the Joy of the Lord is your _____. Nehemiah 8:10
10. God wants our joy to be_____. John 16:24
12. And _____ and nature sing

©Not Consumed 2015 | Gloria: A Christmas Hymn Study

Color the letters of the word JOY. We can have JOY in all things because of what Jesus did for us. Around the word JOY write some things that you can find JOY in because of Jesus.

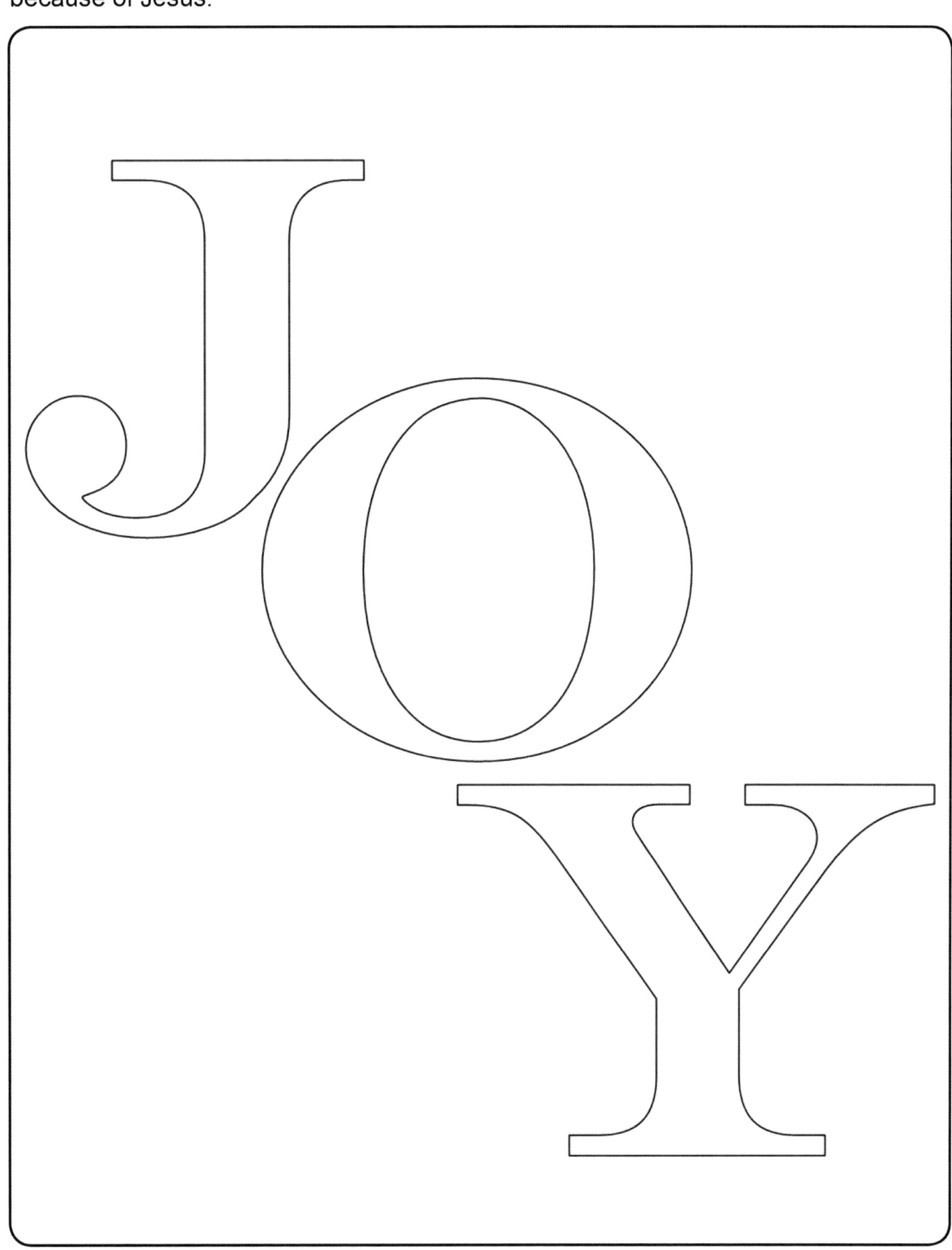

I bring you good tidings of great JOY,
which shall be to all people.
Luke 2:10 KJV

©Not Consumed 2015 | Gloria: A Christmas Hymn Study

In 1857, John Henry Hopkins, Jr. wrote this hymn as part of a Christmas pageant for the General Theological Seminary in New York City, where he was an instructor in church music. Hopkins was a minister, composer, music teacher, and designer of stained glass windows.

Reports say that his purpose was to devise a special Christmas present for his beloved nephews and nieces during his annual holiday trip to his father's home in Vermont. He wrote the song in parts so that each of the wise men could sing his own part.

The song was published in Hopkin's 1863 collection, Carols, Hymns, and Songs, and later in a separately published, specially illustrated 1865 version. Both the 1863 and 1865 publications carried the title "Three Kings of Orient."

This hymn is unique as it's one of the few hymns about the visit of the wise men. Because of this, it became the only American carol to be published in Christmas Carols, New and Old, an 1871 collection that was instrumental in reviving carol collecting and singing in England.

Listen to these beautiful arrangements:
Vocal, Piano, Youth Orchestra

MY HYMN NOTES

Hymn Name
_____

Author
_____

Date Written
_____

Its original language was
_____

Other Facts
_____
_____
_____
_____
_____
_____

Tell a little about the story behind the hymn. You can write and draw.

Text: John H. Hopkins, Jr., 1857
Tune: John H. Hopkins, Jr., 1857

We Three Kings

1. We three kings of O-ri-ent are; bear-ing gifts we tra-verse a-far, field and foun-tain, moor and moun-tain, fol-lo-wing yon-der star.
2. Born a King on Beth-le-hem's plain, gold I bring to crown him a-gain, King for-e-ver, ceas-ing ne-ver, o-ver us all to reign.
3. Frank-in-cense to of-fer have I; in-cense owns a De-i-ty nigh; prayer and prais-ing, voi-ces rais-ing, wor-shi-ping God on high.
4. Myrrh is mine; its bit-ter per-fume breathes a life of ga-the-ring gloom; sor-rowing, sigh-ing, bleed-ing, dy-ing, sealed in the stone-cold tomb.
5. Glo-rious now be-hold him a-rise; King and God and sac-ri-fice: Al-le-lu-ia, Al-le-lu-ia, sounds through the earth and skies.

Refrain

O star of won-der, star of light, star with roy-al beau-ty bright, west-ward lead-ing, still pro-ceed-ing, guide us to thy per-fect light.

88 446 Refrain
KINGS OF ORIENT
www.hymnary.org/text/we_three_kings_of_orient_are

This hymn is in the public domain. You may freely use this score for personal and congregational worship. If you reproduce the score, please credit Hymnary.org as the source.

©Not Consumed 2015 | Gloria: A Christmas Hymn Study

We Three Kings of Orient Are

John Henry Hopkins

COPYWORK

We three kings of Orient are
Bearing gifts we traverse afar
Field and fountain, moor and mountain
Following yonder star
O star of wonder, star of night
Star with royal beauty bright
Westward leading, still proceeding
Guide us to thy perfect light

THE TRUTH ABOUT KINGS

There are many different ideas about these "three kings" who came to see Jesus. Read this article to help you see what the Bible really says about this event. Then draw and write about your findings below.

_____

_____

_____

_____

_____

THE GIFTS

The Bible isn't clear about how many wise men visited Jesus or when they arrived. However, it does say exactly what gifts they brought. Read Matthew 2:1-12 and then answer the questions below. Follow the link to see what each gift looks like and draw a picture in the box.

Gift #1 _____

Gold was usually given to royalty. Why do you think they gave it to Jesus?

_____

_____

_____

Gift #2 _____

Frankincense was used by Jews only to worship God at the altar. Why do you think they gave it to Jesus?
(see Hebrews 10:14-18)

_____

_____

_____

Gift #3 _____

Myrrh was a perfume that was used for special occasions, most often to prepare cloths to bury someone who had died. Why do you think they gave it to Jesus?

_____

_____

_____

MY GIFTS TO JESUS

Read Matthew 2:11 again. Did you notice what they offered before the gifts?

We, too, can really only have one response to the birth of our Savior: worship. What are some ways you can worship Jesus today? (Here are some ideas to get you started.)

1. Sing
2. Pray
3. Read your Bible
4. Obey God
5. Tithe
6. Share the good news
7. Love others
8. Serve others
9. Be thankful
10. Go to church

We end our study with one of the best known hymns from England. The author of the hymn is not known for certain, but it was probably sung for hundreds of years before it was first written down in William Sandy's Christmas Carols Ancient and Modern in 1833. The writer probably didn't publish his name on the hymn because, at the time, church leaders did not accept upbeat and lively hymns such as this one.

By the mid-1800s, Queen Victoria delighted in carols and the tune became much loved across the country and even into the United States. The carol would have been sung by the waits of olden England. Waits were city employees whose duties included singing carols and songs at city events.

The words really don't make sense to us today, but in that time they had significant meaning. "God Rest Ye Merry, Gentlemen" can more accurately be said: "God Make You Mighty, Gentlemen." I love thinking about that. Yes, God sent His son into this world to make us mighty. Mighty to serve Him and resist the enemy!

I think you would agree with the lyrics of this tune. It's the birth of Christ that gives us great TIDINGS OF COMFORT AND JOY!

Listen to beautiful arrangements here:
[Irish Choir](#), [Piano](#), [Canadian Brass](#)

©Not Consumed 2015 | Gloria: A Christmas Hymn Study

MY HYMN NOTES

Hymn Name
_____

Author
_____

Date Written
_____

Its original language was
_____

Other Facts
_____
_____
_____
_____
_____
_____
_____

Tell a little about the story behind the hymn. You can write and draw.

God Rest Ye Merry, Gentlemen

Traditional English Carol

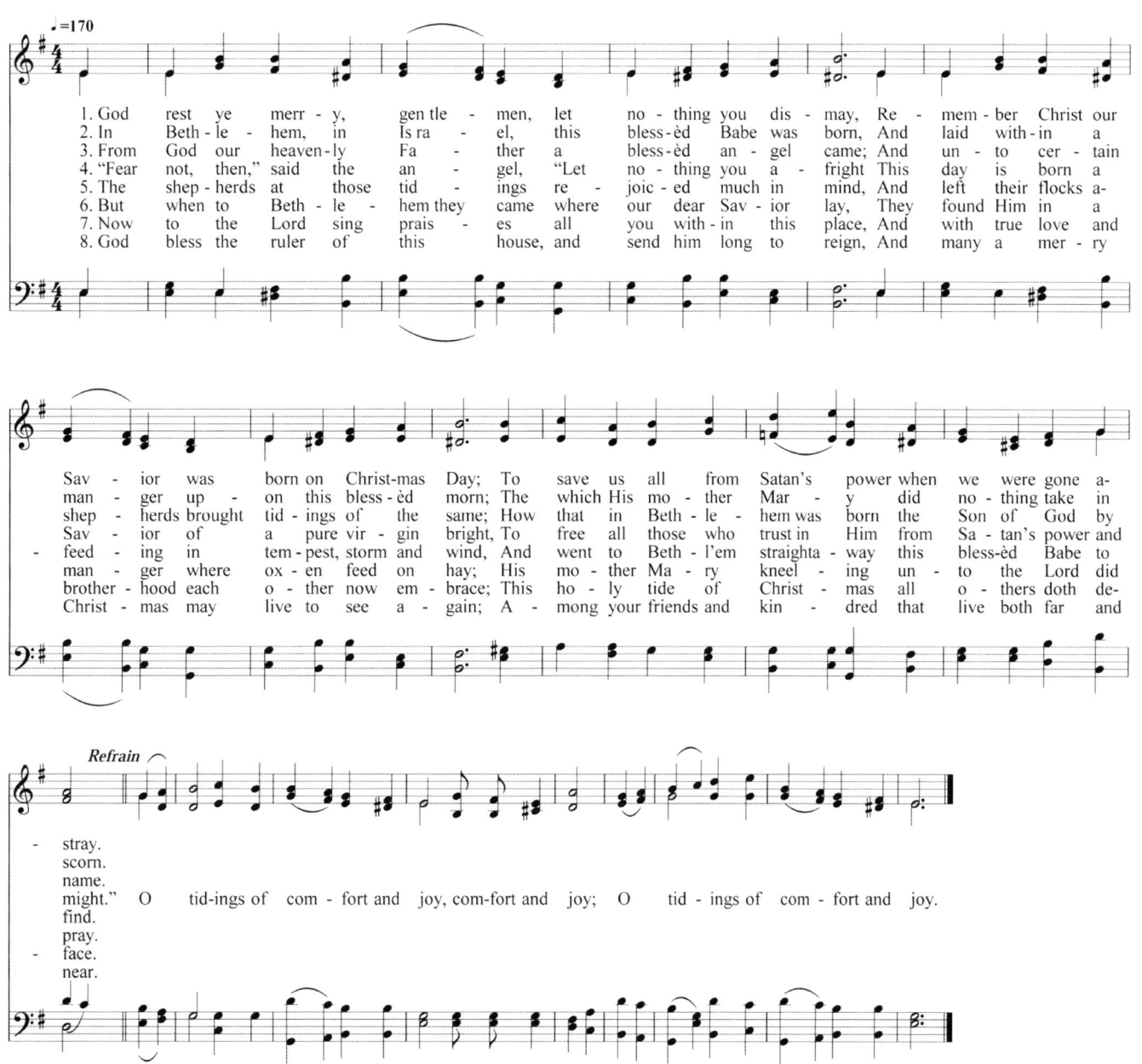

Public Domain
Courtesy of the Cyber Hymnal™

TIN WHISTLE TABLATURE

God Rest Ye Merry, Gentlemen

2
In Bethlehem, in Jewery, This Blessed Babe was born,
And laid within a manger, upon this blessed morn;
That which His mother Mary, did nothing take in scorn,

3
From God our Heav'nly Father, A blessed Angel came;
And unto certain Shepherds, brought tidings of the same;
How that in Bethehem was born the Son of God by name,

COPYWORK

God rest ye merry, gentlemen
Let nothing you dismay
Remember, Christ, our Savior
Was born on Christmas day
To save us all from Satan's power
When we were gone astray
O tidings of comfort and joy
Comfort and joy
O tidings of comfort and joy

THE POWER OF THE CROSS

As we learned, the lyrics in this hymn actually mean "God make you mighty, gentlemen." Did you know that you have mighty power? Let's look in the Bible and see what that means.

Write 2 Timothy 1:7 here:

_____

_____

_____

2 Corinthians 12:9 says that Christ's power _____ upon me.

According to Ephesians 3:20, God's power is

_____.

It's so exciting to think that God's power rests on us and is at work within us! With God, nothing is impossible. He will give us everything we need to do whatever He has called us to do.

Write Philippians 4:13 here:

_____

_____

_____

In Christ, God has given me
_____ _____ _____ _____ _____
to love, obey, and resist the temptation to sin!

Unscramble the words from the hymn.

1. sytaar _____

2. tcshri _____

3. gdniist _____

4. ansat _____

5. tmnegenel _____

6. esrt _____

7. vaes _____

8. pewor _____

9. ogd _____

10. fmrctoo _____

11. cshimrats _____

12. osriav _____

13. rmyre _____

14. ojy _____

15. symadi _____

©Not Consumed 2015 | Gloria: A Christmas Hymn Study

Then spake Jesus again unto them, saying, I am the light of the world: he that followeth me shall not walk in darkness, but shall have the light of life.
John 8:12 (KJV)

©Not Consumed 2015 | Gloria: A Christmas Hymn Study

Again Jesus spoke to them, saying, "I am the light of the world. Whoever follows me will not walk in darkness, but will have the light of life." John 8:12 (ESV)

APPENDIX

Copywork in KJV

Copywork in ESV

COPYWORK

Therefore the Lord himself shall give you a sign; Behold, a virgin shall conceive, and bear a son, and shall call his name Immanuel.
Isaiah 7:14 KJV

COPYWORK

But thou, Bethlehem Ephratah, though thou be little among the thousands of Judah, yet out of thee shall he come forth unto me that is to be ruler in Israel; whose goings forth have been from of old, from everlasting. Micah 5:2 KJV

COPYWORK

And she brought forth her firstborn son, and wrapped him in swaddling clothes, and laid him in a manger; because there was no room for them in the inn. Luke 2:7 KJV

COPYWORK

For unto us a child is born, unto us a son is given: and the government shall be upon his shoulder: and his name shall be called Wonderful, Counsellor, The mighty God, The everlasting Father, The Prince of Peace. Isaiah 9:6 KJV

COPYWORK

And suddenly there was with the angel a multitude of the heavenly host praising God, and saying, Glory to God in the highest, and on earth peace, good will toward men.
Luke 2:13-14 KJV

COPYWORK

And when they were come into the house, they saw the young child with Mary his mother, and fell down, and worshipped him: and when they had opened their treasures, they presented unto him gifts; gold, and frankincense and myrrh. Matthew 2:11 KJV

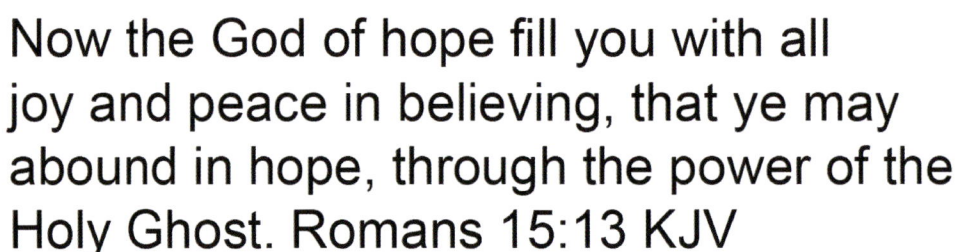

COPYWORK

Now the God of hope fill you with all joy and peace in believing, that ye may abound in hope, through the power of the Holy Ghost. Romans 15:13 KJV

COPYWORK

Therefore the Lord himself will give you a sign. Behold, the virgin shall conceive and bear a son, and shall call his name Immanuel. Isaiah 7:14 ESV

COPYWORK

But you, O Bethlehem Ephrathah, who are too little to be among the clans of Judah, from you shall come forth for me one who is to be ruler in Israel, whose coming forth is from of old, from ancient days. Micah 5:2 ESV

COPYWORK

And she gave birth to her firstborn son and wrapped him in swaddling cloths and laid him in a manger, because there was no place for them in the inn. Luke 2:7 ESV

COPYWORK

For to us a child is born, to us a son is given; and the government shall be upon his shoulder, and his name shall be called Wonderful Counselor, Mighty God, Everlasting Father, Prince of Peace.
Isaiah 9:6 ESV

COPYWORK

And suddenly there was with the angel a multitude of the heavenly host praising God and saying, "Glory to God in the highest, and on earth peace among those with whom he is pleased!" Luke 2:13-14 ESV

COPYWORK

And going into the house they saw the child with Mary his mother, and they fell down and worshiped him. Then, opening their treasures, they offered him gifts, gold and frankincense and myrrh. Matthew 2:11 ESV

COPYWORK

May the God of hope fill you with all joy and peace in believing, so that by the power of the Holy Spirit you may abound in hope. Romans 15:13 ESV

Made in the USA
Charleston, SC
12 November 2016